James H. Parks, James D Cleaver

History of the Scotch Plains Baptist Church

James H. Parks, James D Cleaver

History of the Scotch Plains Baptist Church

ISBN/EAN: 9783337405182

Printed in Europe, USA, Canada, Australia, Japan

Cover: Foto ©Lupo / pixelio.de

More available books at **www.hansebooks.com**

HISTORY

of the

Scotch Plains Baptist Church

from its

Organization on the Fifth of August 1747

to its

One Hundred and Fiftieth Anniversary

on the Fifth of August 1897

❧ ❧

Prepared by

Rev. J. H. Parks, D. D. and Judge James D. Cleaver

and published by the Church

Scotch Plains, New Jersey

• 1897 •

The trustees of the Scotch Plains Baptist Church adopted the following Preamble and Resolutions, Feb. 12, 1896:

"Whereas the One hundred and fiftieth Anniversary of the organization of this Church will arrive in the year of our Lord, one thousand eight hundred and ninety-seven, and will be a period in the history of the Old Church, which ought of right and of gratitude to God, to be marked with suitable and appropriate ceremonies of observance, congratulation and thankfulness;

And, Whereas, in the opinion of this Board, it would be a fitting item of such a celebration to have prepared for permanent preservation a condensed history of the life and prominent events which have marked her career;

Therefore, be it Resolved, that Dr. James H. Parks and Judge James D. Cleaver be, and they are hereby appointed to go over the records of the Church and of this Board from the date of the founding of the Church down to the date of the Anniversary in 1897, and collate and arrange in Chronological order the prominent and interesting events which have come to the Church in her long and eventful career, as the first Standard bearer of religion in this Community—as the Mother of Churches, and as one of the pillars of piety, law, liberty of conscience and civil order for the State.

Resolved, that the paper so prepared shall, when approved by this Board be printed for distribution on the Anniversary day aforesaid; and afterwards, together with the observances of the day be put into a Souvenir volume to be sold to any persons desiring to have them."

3

The Committee have accordingly endeavored to prepare a reliable History as to facts and dates.

They acknowledge valuable help received from the History of Baptists, by Dr. Armitage, The Baptist Encyclopedia by Dr. Cathcart, The Bi-Centennial of the Piscataway Baptist Church, The One hundred and fiftieth Anniversary of the Hightstown Baptist Church, The Minutes of the Philadelphia, New York and East New Jersey Associations; as well as from the memories of some of the older members of the Scotch Plains Church.

HISTORY.

There are many human organizations which have so ennobled humanity and exemplified great principles of truth, that their history deserves to be recorded and perpetuated. Though they were originated by human foresight only, yet their existence and usefulness will ever be held in grateful remembrance.

But the Church of Christ is not a human organization. It is one of the Divine institutions among men. It was divinely organized. Its laws and discipline were divinely enacted. Its officers were divinely appointed and its members are divinely qualified. Hence we come to the study of the history of a Christian Church with a peculiar interest. We are tracing the dealings of God with his people. We are scanning the efficiency of a divinely appointed means, to the accomplishment of its end, and we are recording the degree of faithfulness with which the Church has fulfilled its divinely appointed mission.

The Scotch Plains Baptist Church was organized in August, 1747. This entire region at that time was known as the Province of East New Jersey, and was under the dominion of the King of Great Britain. All of its inhabitants were loyal English subjects. The country was sparsely settled. There were no railroads, nor post offices, nor telegraphs —in fact no public means of transportation, nor of conveying intelligence. The surroundings were so different from those with which we are familiar, that we can scarcely realize them.

There were few Baptist Churches at that time in all that is now known, as the whole State of New Jersey, and these were widely separated. One was situated at Middletown, one at Piscataway, one at Cohansey, one at Cape May, one at Hopewell, one at Kingwood and one organized only two years before, at Hightstown.

There were a number of Baptist families living in this immediate vicinity, and identified with the Piscataway Baptist Church. The distance from and inconveniences in reaching their church home, induced them to ask for letters of dismission in order to organize a church at this place. Their application was answered by the following resolution adopted by the parent church at Piscataway.

"Whereas, in the course of Divine Providence there is necessity of a church to be constituted at the Scotch Plains, in the County of Essex, in East New Jersey, and some of the members of the Baptist Church at Piscataway in the County of Middlesex and the Province aforesaid. having their dwellings at and near the said Scotch Plains, and they having made application to us, and obtained a grant for a dismission from us, in order to incorporate themselves into a church; this may certify that William Darby. Recompense Stanbery, John Lambert John Dennis, John Stanbery, Henry Crosby, John Sutton Jr., Isaac Manning, Mary Brodwell, Mary Green, Mary Dennis, Tabitha Sutton, Catherine Manning, Sarah De Camp and Sarah Perce, when they are regularly constituted into a church according to gospel order and given themselves up, in a church fellowship are fully and freely dismissed from our church."

THE ORGANIZATION.

Accordingly on the fifth day of August, 1747, these brethren and sisters met and resolved to become and be a Regular Baptist Church. They adopted and signed a solemn covenant. Some of the terms of which were, that they humbly accepted Jesus Christ as High Priest, Lawgiver and Savior. That they trusted implicitly and only in his atoning blood and sovereign grace for Salvation—that they would walk together in all holiness, godliness, humility and brotherly love—that they would watch over one another for good—that they would pray with and for one another and for the church—that they would bear one another's burdens, bear with one another's weaknesses as Christ had enjoined and set the example—that they would strive together for the truth of the gospel, and to observe and guard the ordinances in their purity, and would give according to their ability to maintain the Cause of the Master.

Thus the church was organized by these our honored forefathers upon the true foundation, Jesus Christ himself being the chief Corner Stone, and every distinguishing characteristic of our denomination separately referred to in the Covenant Compact. Surely if any people have reason to rejoice in the inheritance left by the forefathers, we may thank God, that the Constituent members of our Zion occupied no compromising ground, and blew no uncertain blast, concerning either the doctrines or practices of the christian church.

These constituent members have all long since passed away, but many of their descendants and the families they represent are still among us, honored and respected members of the community.

7

The organization also included the election by the body of Samuel Drake as Church Clerk, and William Darby and Recompense Stanbery as Ruling Elders, and as the record declares were also to perform the duties of Deacons. Thus the church was duly constituted and publicly recognized and fellowshipped as a Regular Baptist Church.

REV. MR. MILLER'S PASTORATE.

Soon after the organization, the church extended a call to Benjamin Miller, a member of the Piscataway Church to become their Pastor. This call Mr. Miller accepted and was ordained to the ministry, by request of this church, by Rev. Benjamin Stelle of Piscataway, Rev. James Carman of Cranbery and Abel Morgan of Middletown.

The Church immediately united with the Philadelphia Association.

Of the antecedents of Rev. Mr. Miller, little is positively known. It is probable that he was converted to God some ten years before by means of the ministry of Rev. Gilbert Tennant a celebrated Presbyterian minister of New Brunswick, N. J., and united with the Piscataway Baptist Church. Here his ability and zeal were noticed and commended, and he was readily granted a license to preach the Gospel of Jesus Christ.

After becoming pastor of this church he evinced especial qualifications for the work. The infant organization was to be nursed, developed and strengthened. Baptists who were not already identified with it were to be visited and to be made interested in the new enterprise. Unconverted souls were to be instructed in the way of Salvation.

All this work must have required an especial adaptation and a peculiar energy. His labors were not confined to this immediate vicinity, but he gave all the strength of his early manhood to the performance of his divinely appointed mission. He frequently travelled, of course only by the slow means of transportation of his time, to various sections of this and neighboring provinces, carrying the bread of life to the needy, and instructing and comforting the feeble churches. The result of such labor with the blessing of God was soon apparent. The congregations increased. The membership was enlarged, and growth and development was visible on every hand. This is apparent from the fact recorded in the minutes, that it became necessary to enlarge the house of worship in the year, 1758.

It is probable that a meeting house had been erected previous to the organization of the church. But this had become too small for their accommodation during these first eleven years of active united labor. Hence on August 12th, 1758 it was voted "to enlarge the meeting house, to cover it with cedar shingles both roof and sides and to finish it well both outside and inside." A committee consisting of Recompense Stanbery, John Stites, Captain Drake and Captain McDonnel were appointed to complete this improvement. Thus with increased facilities and "an enlarged place of their tent" the church grew both in numbers and in influence.

Rev. Mr. Miller seems to have been indefatigable in preaching the word, enforcing the discipline, and watching over the interests of the now well established Zion. He appears to have had peculiar executive ability, and could readily discover what was best to do, and lead the people to do it. He had access to their ears, their affections and to their contributions; and he made use of all, not for his own aggrandizement, or to secure for himself a name, but for the glory of God and the progress of the Cause of the Master.

There was at this time no Regular Baptist Church in New York City. There were a number of Baptists there who were members of the Fishkill Baptist Church, and elsewhere. These being recommended to do so, united themselves in church relationship with this church and were frequently visited by Rev. James Carman pastor of the Cranbery church (now Hightstown) and by Rev. Mr. Miller, who by authority of the Scotch Plains Church regularly administered the Communion once every quarter, and baptised when necessary. The congregations there increased so that no private dwelling house could accomodate them, and they found it necessary to hire a rigging loft in Cart and Horse Street, now William St. where they held their meetings for a number of years. They then erected their first church edifice on Gold Street. On the 19th of June 1762 twenty seven persons, namely, John Carman, Jeremiah Dodge, Andrew Thompson, Samuel Edmonds, John Degray, Elias Baylis, Jos. Meeks, Wm. Colegrove, Samuel Dodge, Catharine Degray, Mary Stillwell, Hannah Hayton, Hannah French, Mary Murphy, Margaret Dodge, Sarah Meeks, Sarah Thompson, Jane Calwell, Mary Edmonds, Susannah Mires, Ruth Perine, Mary Smith, Eliza VanDike, Mary Simmons, Rachel Williams and Catherine Leonard who had received letters of dismission for the purpose from this church organized the First Regular Baptist Church of New York City. On the same day Rev. John Gano, also of this church, became Pastor of the new organization, and held the position for twenty-six eventful years.

After the lapse of five more years of labor and success, it became advisable to organize a Baptist church at Mount Bethel, N. J. The members living in that vicinity were united with this church, but in order to attend divine worship, it was necessary for them to ride from six to ten miles over rough hilly roads. As soon as they became strong enough they requested letters of dismission in order to constitute a new centre of religious influence more convenient to their own homes. This request was readily granted, and on the 2nd day of Sept. 1767 letters of dismission were given to eight males and ten females namely, Benjamin Sutton, Benj. Sutton Jr., Abram Sutton, David Jennings, William Worth, John Pound, John Worth, James Sutton, Elizabeth Tingley, Hannah Coon, Mary Sutton, Rosannah Cowart, Anna Worth, Lois Sutton, Dinah Worth, Etta Worth, Patience Bloom, and Elizabeth Hayden. The church was organized; and they have been a prosperous and sucessful agency for the advancement of the Redeemer's Cause.

The Lyons Farms Baptist Church was organized from the Scotch Plains church in the year 1769. Eleven members namely, Ezekiel Crane, Ichabod Grummon, Loftus Grummon, Jos. Meeker, Jos. Gildersleeve, Samuel Smith, Jonathan Tompkins, Mary Meeker, Abegail Crane, Johannah Grummon and Jerusha Crane were dismissed for that purpose on the 29th day of March. This church has been united and successful and still maintain their visibility and usefulness. Thus in a period of only twenty two years, three churches were organized directly from this church, and yet the Scotch Plains Church numbered One hundred and five happy united efficient members, who probably presented an array of moral and pecuniary strength not excelled by any church at the time.

During Rev. Mr. Miller's pastorate several periods of special gathering were enjoyed, among which was a revival in the year 1768 when the names of forty-eight persons are recorded as being baptised into the church fellowship. This result seems to have been acomplished by the use of the ordinary means of grace, as the minutes make no mention of any foreign aid to the pastor, nor of any extra religious services.

Among those who were baptised by Rev. Benjamin Miller were several who became prominent in the service of the Master, and eminently useful in the upbuilding of our denomination in this remote period of its history. One of these was James Manning, who was the son of Isaac Manning, one of the constituent members of this church. About the age of eighteen years he went to Hopewell, N. J. to prepare for college, under the instruction of Rev. Isaac Eaton. In 1758 he was baptised into the fellowship of this church, and in the same year entered the College of New Jersey now Princeton University, where he graduated with honors in 1762. Shortly after his graduation he was ordained to the ministry at Scotch Plains. Rev. John Gano of New York, preached the ordination sermon, Rev. Isaac Eaton of Hopewell gave the charge, and Rev. Isaac Stelle of Piscataway offered the ordaining prayer. He then spent a year in travelling extensively through the country having previously married a daughter of John Stites. In 1764 he removed to Warren, about ten miles from Providence, R. I. where he established a grammar school which soon became a flourishing institution. A church was organized in Warren the same year, and Mr. Manning was called to the pastorate. A charter was also obtained from the General Assembly, authorizing the establishment of the College of Rhode Island, and in 1765 Mr. Manning was formally appointed President of the College, and Professor of Languages "with full power to act in these capacities at Warren or elsewhere." In 1770 it was determined to remove the College from Warren to Providence, the town and county subscribing £4200 as an inducement thereto. Mr. Manning resigned the care of the church at Warren, but was almost immediately called to the pastorate of the First Baptist Church at Providence. President Manning continued his multifarious duties as President, Professor and Pastor until the breaking out of the war of the Revolution. The College had been growing in reputation and usefulness, and was fast attaining the high position and influence it now occupies as Brown University. All through the revolutionary struggle Mr. Manning succeeded in keeping the institution intact, though "University Hall" was occupied much of the time by the British Soldiers as Barracks, and it was not until 1782 that the course of instruction was permanently resumed. Indeed so identified with the life of James Manning was the history of Brown University, that the story of the earlier years of that Institution is also the story of his life. President Manning feeling that his collegiate duties were too great to allow him to give

to the church the care it required, in 1791 requested the appointment of a successor; but before the
request had been complied with, he was stricken
with apoplexy and his useful life ended July 29,
1791, in the fifty-third year of his age.

Thus Rev. Mr. Miller's pastorate was blessed of
God, not only in the building up of this church,
and in the establishing of three other churches;
but in the raising up of men who became lights in
both the literary and religious world.

Mr. Miller served the church about thirty-four
years, and died on the 14th day of November,
1781, and was buried by the loving hands of his
people in the burying ground which surrounded
the church edifice where he had so long and so
earnestly preached the gospel. His sepulchre is
with us to this day, and it is and ought to be held
by the church as a sacred trust of all that is mortal
of him who in the providence of God was the
pioneer pastor of our beloved Zion. He left one
son and four daughters who resided in the homestead on the farm now owned by our honored
townsman, A. D. Sheperd, Esq.

For more than four years after the death of Mr.
Miller the church was without direct pastoral
oversight. Mr. Runi Runyon supplied the pulpit
half of the time for a few months and Mr. Benjamin Coles upon invitation of the church, became a
stated supply. He served the church faithfully
for about two years, but no marked display of the
divine favor, seemed to attend his labors. The
church were much discouraged, as is apparent
from their letter to the Association at Philadelphia
Oct. 5, 1784, in which they request "Counsel, Assistance and Supplies as the Association in their

wisdom shall think most proper" adding "we are at peace among ourselves, though much deadness still prevails; many minding their own things, and but few the things that are Jesus Christ's."

After this a George Guthrie, as his recommendation declares "a young brother not long since from Ireland" visited the church; but he only remained about five months and then removed to Morristown.

REV. MR. VAN HORN'S PASTORATE.

On the 15th of December, 1785, Rev. William Van Horn accepted a call to the pastorate. He was a young man thirty-eight years of age, of Buck's County, Pennsylvania. He graduated from the Academy of Dr. Samuel Jones, at Lower Dublin, Pa. During the revolutionary war he had been a chaplain in the army, enthusiastically encouraging the heroes who fought against tyranny, and cheering them on in their toilsome marches, while sharing with them their greatest dangers and most grievous hardships. He had also been a pastor at Southhampton some thirteen years. His preaching is said to have been "of the most solid and instructive character, never descending into careless frivolity, but always with becoming gravity as a messenger from the throne of God, declaring the will of the Most High to men."

His ministry here like that of his predecessor proved eminently sucessful. The first year he baptised forty-seven persons; and these as the minutes reveal after the closest examination and scrutiny. The whole number baptised during his pastorate was one hundred and sixty. While he evinced great pulpit power, he also had an executive ability, which made his pastoral work a success.

Previous to the coming of Mr. Van Horn, indeed, as early as 1761, what was called a *vestry* was organized, consisting of seven men, who seem to have had especial control of the temporal affairs of the church. Mr. Van Horn formulated a plan for connecting the church and congregation, for the support of the Gospel and the care of the temporal interests of the Society. Whatever the plan was (for the minutes do not record it) it was adopted and continued in operation until February, 1788, when, in accordance with a law passed by the Legislature in 1786, for incorporating religious societies, seven Trustees were chosen and a certificate of incorporation was filed in the Clerk's office in Newark. In 1869, this incorporation was confirmed as an especial charter by Act of the Legislature; the trustees being clothed with power to sell lands.

During Mr. Van Horn's administration two churches were constituted directly from the membership of this.

In the spring of 1788, three brothers, Abraham Drake, Cornelius Drake and Isaac Drake, and two brothers-in-law John Shotwell and David Morris, were induced by the glowing descriptions of Rev. William Wood, pastor of the Baptist church at Washington, Kentucky, to leave their homes here and seek their fortunes in the wilds of the West. These brethren with their wives, children and effects were accompanied by Rev. John Gano, who was then moving his all from the City of New York. They sailed down the Ohio River to Limestone, where they landed and proceeded at once to

Washington, four miles distant. Here they made a temporary stay until they could select a site upon which to settle. In the early fall, they bought from a Mr. May a tract of land containing fourteen hundred acres, eight miles west of Washington. They made an equitable division of their land according to the amount of money each had put into the common stock, and in such a manner, that the lot of each had a corner in a Salt spring. Around this spring they built their log houses, and established their colony, calling the incipient village *May's Lick*.

Before leaving their home the aforesaid brethren with their wives had been granted letters of dismission from this church, on the 12th of April, 1788. Hence, as soon as convenient they organized themselves into a Particular Baptist Church at May's Lick, Ky., on November 28, 1789. Rev. William Wood of Washington, Ky., and James Garrard, who afterward for two terms was Governor of the State, were the officiating ministers on the occasion. Thus the Scotch Plains church became the mother of a child in what was then regarded as the far west.

The May's Lick church grew in numbers, and religious power and influence, until in 1889 at their centennial anniversary, they are reported as one of the strongest churches, and centers of evangelizing progress in that part of the west.

The other church organized during the pastorate of Rev. Mr. Van Horn, was the one at Samptown in our immediate vicinity.

On the 21st of August, 1792, letters of dismission were given to Christianns Lupordus, Samuel Drake and wife, Peter Till, Joseph Randolph,

Benjamin Blackford, Dugal Ayers, Ephraim F. Randolph and wife, Joseph Manning, Robert Randolph, Mary Blackford, Joseph Drake, John Luke, Margaret Luke, George Laying, Zervia Manning, Unis Cole and Morris Frazee. Accordingly on the 1st of December, 1792, the Samptown Baptist Church was constituted—being about midway between this place and Piscataway, the pastors of both churches had preached there with some regularity. But as it was manifestly better that they should have an organization of their own, they were set apart as a gospel church— David Jones of Southampton, Pa., and Jacob F. Randolph taking part in the Services. This church, too, recently held their centennial exercises showing commendable progress and efficiency.

After Mr. Van Horn had accepted the pastorate, but probably before he had removed his family to this place, the Parsonage, a frame building which stood nearer the street than the present one, was consumed by fire early in 1786. It was immediately determined to rebuild; and as there was some difference of opinion about where the new building should stand, after determining that it should be constructed of stone, it was voted "to indulge Mr. Van Horn with his choice." He wisely chose the present location, and during that year all the stone part of the present building was erected under the pastor's immediate supervision: and every pastor who has occupied it since has had occasion to commend the wisdom and foresight of his plans.

Mr. Van Horn served the church well and faithfully for nearly twenty-two years. He gained and held the respect and confidence, not only of this church, but of the denomination at large. His family were amiable and intelligent, a consolation to himself and an ornament to the community. But in the latter part of his ministry, his health failed, and he, having quite a large tract of land in the southwestern part of Ohio, determined to resign his pastorate and to remove thither. Hence, on the 28th day of September, 1807, he and his family entered the wagons which were to convey him from the scenes of twenty years of happy associations with a loving people. The long tedious journey increased his maladies, and he was only able to reach Pittsburg, Pa., where, on the 31st of October, he passed away to his eternal home. The people of Pittsburg sympathized with the afflicted family and showed them many kind attentions. After the funeral the widow and children pursued their journey to their destination.

The church were without a pastor about nine months, during which time they were supplied by Jacob F. Randolph and Henry Ball, both members of the church and baptised by Rev. Mr. Van Horn and licensed to preach the gospel.

PASTORATE OF THOMAS BROWN.

In March, 1808, at the invitation of a committee appointed by the church, Rev. Thomas Brown, Pastor of the Baptist church at Salem, N. J., visited this church. The labors of Mr. Brown and his visit were highly enjoyed, and the following April, a unanimous call was extended to him to become Pastor. This call he accepted, and removed to this place July 1, 1808. Mr. Brown, was a native of Newark, N. J. At the age of seventeen years he was converted, and united with the First Presbyterian Church of that city. His evident preaching talent and inclination, led his friends to advise him to prepare for the ministry. He had not proceeded far in his preparations, when a complete change of views compelled him to be baptised and become a member of the First Baptist Church of Newark. Afterward, he spent some years in study, chiefly under the supervision of Dr. Samuel Jones, and in 1805, assumed his first charge at Salem, where he was ordained as Pastor. Dr. Staughton and Dr. Jones, officiated at his ordination. He remained at Salem about three years, when he came to this place at the call of the church. His pastoral relations were pleasant and harmonious from the beginning. His pulpit ministrations as well as his judicious and efficient pastoral labors were highly appreciated. Baptisms were reported every year, with only one exception, the whole number amounting to one hundred and fifty, even though the most careful scrutiny was observed in the examination of candidates. Mr. Brown was amiable and cheerful in private life, and held in high esteem for his social qualities; but his especial power was in his pulpit ministrations. These were always instructive and interesting, and often especially eloquent and thrilling. His management of cases of discipline was tenderly wise and judiciously strict, and thus he endeared himself to the church membership and to the community.

In the winter of 1816-'17, the meeting house, which had no doubt been built before the organization of the church, and stood on ground a short distance Northwest of the present edifice, was accidently burned and totally destroyed—of course all the inhabitants turned out to witness the unwelcome conflagration. Among others who were present was Recompense Stanbery, the son of the first deacon of the church and the father of our esteemed townsman William C. Stanbery. While the flames were consuming the timbers of the revered old structure, Mr. Stanbery said: "Brethren there is no better time to resolve to rebuild than now, as we stand around these smouldering embers." He then announced his own subscription for the purpose. His example was contagious, one and another followed, and a considerable portion of the amount needed for the new house was raised then and there. Before the beginning of the new year, work was commenced and a new edifice, larger than the former one was erected. Recompense Stanbery, Joseph Bradford, John B. Osborn, Samuel B. Miller and David Osborn were the building committee who superintended the work to its completion. The new building cost about three thousand dollars and was paid for by contributions received almost exclusively from this vicinity, though the First Church of New York City sent some assistance to her mother in her time of need. There is little doubt that the spot upon which the new house was built was the same as that upon which the old one had stood, and that that ground had been donated to the church by William Darby, its first Ruling Elder; and consisted of five square chains, comprising the entire old burying ground. The other lands possessed by the church at this time was what was known as "the parsonage farm," and consisted of fifteen acres on the Plains, and twelve acres on the mountain. This had been purchased of the executors of William Darby in 1775, and had been occupied by each of the succeeding pastors since that time. During the pastorage of Mr. Brown, Deacon James Brown left a legacy to the church, of Twelve hundred dollars, for the support of the poor, which was sacredly used for that purpose for many years.

Thus as time went on, the church was being enriched both spiritually and materially. Rev. Mr. Brown was giving the strength of his manhood to the preaching of Christ crucified. Sinners were being converted, and uniting themselves with this church, while the brotherhood were being cemented in closer fraternal relations by their trials and sorrows as well as their successes.

In November, 1828, much to the regret of his attached people, Mr. Brown resigned the pastorate and removed to Great Valley, Pa. More than twenty years of constant service bore testimony to the faithfulness of the Pastor, but the records of eternity only can reveal the full measure of his success.

PASTORATE OF REV. MR. ROGERS.

After a period of less than a year, the church extended a call to Rev. John Rogers on the 30th of May, 1829. Mr. Rogers was born in the north of Ireland in 1783. He was converted at the age of seventeen years, and united with the Presbyterian Church of which his parents were members. Convinced of a personal call to the ministry, he entered upon a course of study, which was completed at the University of Edinburg. After this he labored among the Independents in Scotland and in Ireland. In the year 1811, after a careful study of the subject, he became convinced that christian baptism is the immersion of a believer in water on profession of faith; and he was thereupon baptised by Rev. Daniel Cook, a Baptist Minister of Scotland. In the year 1816 he came to this country, and after a short residence at Hopewell, N. J., he was called to Pemberton, where he was ordained in 1817. His labors at Pemberton were highly appreciated by the members of that church, and the writer, who afterward labored in the same church, often heard him affectionately spoken of. He continued to labor with the Pemberton church until he removed to this place about the middle of August, 1829.

Mr. Rogers was a close student, and a good and instructive preacher. He had an extensive knowledge of the teachings of the bible, and his views of the plan of Salvation were clear, scriptural and definite. His ministry here was blessed with two special revivals, during which many were brought into the fold of Christ. Among these were three of his own daughters who proved the genuineness of their profession by a humble and pious deportment. Mr. Rogers baptized about one hundred and thirteen happy, rejoicing converts while he labored in this pastorate. The ingathering of 1837 was especially thorough and widespread. Perhaps the gloom and depression of that memorable time of financial distress had something to do with turning men's minds into religious channels and leading to so many similar displays of the power of Divine Grace.

Mr. Rogers took a lively interest in both Home and Foreign Missionary enterprises, and he established in the church a schedule of systematic contributions to these objects.

The New Jersey Baptist State Convention was organized in 1830, and Mr. Rogers was one of its constituent members and gave it his influence during his life.

Mr. Rogers resigned in June, 1841, and removed to Perth Amboy, where he remained only about three years. Thence he went to Paterson, where he spent the remainder of his days without a direct pastoral charge, but preaching frequently and always acceptably for neighboring churches. He died August 30th, 1849, aged sixty-six years. His son, A. C. Rogers, M. D., survives him, and is a prominent and useful worker in the denomination.

These four pastors, who occupied the pulpit of this church nearly the whole of the first century of its existence, were eminent men of God, and their record evinces how certainly the Great Head of the church will raise up suitable and qualified leaders to conduct his people along the line of His own purposes.

All of these men seem to have been wholly consecrated to the work to which God had called them. They knew the truth in their own experience, and they never hesitated to proclaim the doctrines of grace. They loved the distinguishing principles of our denomination, and they taught them fearlessly. Such teachings with the Divine blessing would be apt to make staunch, stalwart, Baptist christians; and it did—all honor to the human agencies—all praise to the Divine leader.

REV. THOMAS F. BROWN, D.D.

REV. MR. WIVELL'S PASTORATE.

John Wivell was born in England. He became a sailor in early life, professed conversion and joined the Methodists—afterward he became a Presbyterian, and among them commenced preaching. He labored sometime in Nova Scotia, and then came to New York and was baptised by Rev. Duncan Dunbar. He was almost immediately licensed and ordained, and spent some time laboring among the seamen. He removed to Scotch Plains in March, 1842, and such was his tact, and insinuating address, that he soon attracted to him the public favor, and the congregation rapidly increased in numbers, and there were many professed converts.

The deportment of Mr. Wivell was regarded by some from the beginning, as somewhat offensive to good taste, but was readily excused on account of his sea-faring life. After a while, reports unfavorable to his moral purity were whispered about. At length the truth burst upon the church like a thunder clap. The humiliation and mortification which ensued was great, and Mr. Wivell was speedily excluded from the fellowship of the church. His subsequent life and the fictitious names he assumed fully proved the wisdom of the church in its prompt action. Nothing so disastrous had ever occurred in the history of the church; but while it humbled the membership, it did not divide them.

The unfortunate incident proves that God's real people will be true and united even under disastrous circumstances; and that the acts of even bad men will be overruled to accomplish His glory.

REV. MR. LOCKE'S PASTORATE.

William E. Locke was a native of New York City. He was baptised by Rev. Dr. Cone in 1831. He was licensed by the Sandy Ridge Baptist church, N. J., in 1833. He was ordained at Moscow, New York, in 1836. He had also been settled at Gouveneur, Trumansburg and Sing Sing, N. Y. He accepted a call to this church and removed to Scotch Plains, May 2d, 1844.

Mr. Locke found the church in the peculiar circumstances resulting from the defection of the former pastor. The labor to be performed was of that kind which needed much adroitness and cool judgment. If Mr. Locke had possessed and exhibited these qualifications it would have been far better for the church. But the course he pursued and the measures he adopted only alienated the membership and increased the friction which already existed. The ingatherings which had marked former pastorates, did not occur. But four persons were added by baptism during Mr. Locke's administration.

On the 8th of August, 1847, the church held a centennial service, commemorating with gratitude the way in which the Head of the church had led them during the first one hundred years of their history. Mr. Locke, preached a centennial discourse on the occasion, which was printed and is in possession of many members of the church, and is held by them in high esteem.

At its organization the church had united with the Philadelphia Association, and in 1792, it had withdrawn and united with the then organized New York Association, and now in 1844, it united with the East New Jersey Association where it has since remained.

Mr. Locke, continued in charge of the church until September 1st, 1849, when he resigned and accepted a call to Amenia, N. Y. He afterward joined the Presbyterian denomination.

REV. MR. RUE'S PASTORATE.

Joshua E. Rue was born at Hightstown, N. J. He was licensed by that church in 1844. He was ordained at Jacobstown as Pastor in 1845, having been educated at Lafayette College and Madison University. Subsequently he served as Pastor at Sandy Ridge, N. J. In the beginning of the year 1850, he accepted a call to the pastorate of this Church and entered upon his duties. He preached the simple doctrines of grace, and as a result, a pleasant condition of spiritual awakening followed, and twenty-seven rejoicing converts were buried in baptism.

But in the midst of his work he was smitten by disease, and for many weeks his life seemed to hang in the balance. He was partially restored however, but was almost immediately called to follow to the grave the remains of his beloved companion, who had also endeared herself to this people. Thus sorely afflicted and with ruined health, he resigned the charge of the church, having served it acceptably just four years. Afterward he held agencies for the Home Mission Society, American Bible Union and for Peddie Institute. He retired to North Carolina, and died in 1887, and his remains were brought to this place and buried beside his wife and near the grave of the first pastor of the church, Benjamin Miller. The Ladies' Circle of this church erected a monument to mark the spot; and the trustees have recently reserved and set apart some adjacent lots for the burial of any who may have served the church as pastor with their immediate families in all time.

During the period of Mr. Rue's pastorate some improvements were made upon the church property.

The number of members in 1854 was one hundred and forty-six.

DR. BROWN'S PASTORATE.

James F. Brown was born in Scotch Plains, July 4th, 1819. He was the son of Rev. Thomas Brown, who was at that time pastor of this church. James F. graduated from the University of Pennsylvania in 1841, and studied theology with Rev. Dr. Dagg. He was ordained Pastor of the Ganisville Baptist Church, Alabama, and in 1846 took charge of the Great Valley church, Pa., where he remained eight years, and was then called to this his native town and to the pastorate of the church his father had so acceptably served. He removed to this place in 1854 and remained six years. He is a man of scholarly attainments, gentle spirit, sound theological views, large sympathies and has been blessed in his ministry. The church during his pastoral connection was harmonious and grew both in numbers and in influence. That memorable year of financial adversity, 1857, was one of spiritual prosperity in this church. Many who were then added became prominent members, and those who yet remain remember gratefully and affectionately the judicious measures and

REV. WILLIAM LUKE.

devout earnestness of the Pastor. Mr. Brown resigned in 1860 and became Pastor at Bridgton, N. J. While at Bridgton the University at Lewisburg honored him with the degree of Doctor of Divinity, and also elected him to the chancellorship of that Institution. Dr. Brown is still living, and although not a Pastor, in consequence of ill health, is held in high esteem in the Denomination.

REV. MR. LUKE'S PASTORATE.

Rev. William Luke was born in Esopus, New York, in 1821. He was both baptized and licensed to preach the gospel at Poughkeepsie, N. Y. He entered Madison University in 1848, but remained only two years when he went to Rochester, where he graduated in 1854. He went to the Province of New Brunswick, but remained only a short time and returned to his native and more congenial climate. He was ordained at Hornellsville, and soon after removed to Forestville, N. Y., where. he preached until 1857. Afterward he became Pastor of the Eighty-third Street Baptist Church of New York City, where during four years of service he was successful in building up the church which was weak when he assumed charge. In 1860 he was called to the pastorate of this church, and having accepted he removed to this place about the first of December of the same year. The circumstances which led; to the war of the Rebellion were culminating. Heated political discussion, was rife on every hand. Pastors were censured, some for being too pronounced in their devotion to the Union cause, and others for being too little so. Mr. Luke took a lively interest in the events transpiring and a number felt aggrieved. The congregation, the membership and the influence of the Pastor, all declined. A number left the church by letter, and only two baptisms occurred during the six years of Mr. Luke's administration. It was at this period too that the church at Westfield was organized, and nearly twenty members asked for and received letters to unite with that organization—all these concurrent circumstances reduced the membership to one hundred and five.

Mr. Luke resigned January 1st, 1867, having been called to Greenport, L. I. Here he labored with much success, but ill-health compelled him to resign the pastorate; and he died at Wappinger Falls, N. Y., in the triumphs of faith, and the hope of the Gospel he had so faithfully preached, on May 16, 1869.

PASTORATE OF DR. BUCHANAN.

Joseph C. Buchanan was born in Ringoes, N. J., in 1841. He entered the sophomore class of Madison University in October, 1863, taking the degree of A. M., in course, three years later. He accepted a call to this church in 1867, and was ordained here, Oct. 1st of that year. Rev. D. J. Yerkes, D. D., of Plainfield, preached on the occasion, and Rev. J. D. Morell delivered the charge to the candidate, and Rev. L. O. Grenell to the church. He remained here until September 1st, 1878, when he resigned this his first pastorate, to accept the call of the Pemberton Baptist Church, where he still remains. During his pastorate at Pemberton, Bucknell University at Lewisburg, Pa., conferred upon him the honorary degree of Doctor of Divinity.

REV. J. C BUCHANAN, D.D.

Dr. Buchanan is a good theologian, a thoughtful preacher, a judicious, affectionate pastor, and has been prospered in winning souls. When he assumed charge of this church a pleasant state of religious feeling met the pastor at the outset; and by a faithful preaching of the gospel, attended by the blessing of God, a most important work of grace was experienced in the year 1868. Nearly fifty were baptised, and many who are now tried and true members of 'the church were converted and put on Christ in baptism as the fruit of his ministry here.

An important material work accomplished during the pastorate of Dr. Buchanan was the erection of our present house of worship. The old church edifice was sold. A considerable part of the parsonage farm was sold for building lots, and a substantial structure was erected on a fine corner, near where the old building stood. The present house is fifty feet by one hundred and ten feet including the lecture room in the rear. The main audience room is fifty by seventy feet with recess pulpit. The building is gothic in style, with corner tower and spire. The material is pressed brick, with Ohio stone and white brick trimmings, and slate roof. The cost including furniture and organ, was Thirty thousand dollars. The removal of the railroad further from the village, thus preventing the increase of population, which was confidently expected, together with the financial depression of the times left the church heavily involved in debt, which rested wearily upon them for many years.

Dr. Buchanan, labored self-sacrificingly and well, and very many members of the church as well as of the community hold him in highest regard. He is actively engaged in furthering the religious interests of our State, as well as our own denominational interests in addition to those of his pastorate. While Dr. Buchanan, is a New Jersey-man, yet his constant effort is for the widest dissemination of gospel truth. May he long live to witness the results of his labors.

PASTORATE OF REV. MR. GUISCARD.

Uriah B. Guiscard, was born and educated in England. In this country he was Pastor at Banks-ville, N. Y., at New London, Conn., at Brewsters, N. Y., and at Greenport, L. I. In each of these places he made a good record. He was called to the pastorate of this church April 29, 1879, and accepted the position early in August of the same year.

During his pastorate the church lost by death three tried and honored deacons, viz.: Jared S. Stout, Henry Hetfield and L. H. K. Smalley. Only two persons were baptised here by Bro. Guis-card. He resigned his charge March 26, 1882. During his administration a fine toned bell was placed in the tower of the church mainly by his efforts. The cemetery also was surrounded with a neat iron fence. Mr. Guiscard, was a good preacher, and had many amiable qualities. After his resignation he settled at Newton, N. J., where he remained a few years. He died, and was buried from the home of his son in Summit, N. J., at the age of seventy-one years.

REV. U. B. GUISCARD.

PASTORATE OF REV. DR. PARKS.

PREPARED BY JUDGE J. D. CLEAVER.

James H. Parks was born in the City of New York, July 13, 1829. He was converted in the year 1847, and united with the Reformed Dutch Church. Soon after he commenced a course of preparation for Rutgers' College, having the Ministry in view, but health failing, and a series of circumstances arising which brought the subject of Christian Baptism to his attention, he was compelled to make a thorough examination of Scriptural teachings upon the subject, which resulted in his being immersed, on profession of faith, on the second day of July, 1854.

He afterward pursued a post-graduate course at Columbian College, Washington, D. C., and received the Degree of Master of Arts, upon Examination, from that Institution.

He was also honored with the Degree of A.M. from Princeton College, New Jersey.

He was ordained to the Ministry, May 28, 1856.

He has been Pastor of the Baptist Churches at Stamford, Connecticut; Bedford, New York; Pemberton, New Jersey; Mannayunk, Pa., and Norwich, Conn.; Calvary, Philadelphia, Pennsylvania; Linden Avenue, Dayton, Ohio, and Scotch Plains, New Jersey.

While Pastor at Scotch Plains, in the year 1889, he received the Degree of D.D. from Shurtliff College, Illinois.

He settled with the Scotch Plains Church the second week in January in the year 1883, and resigned the pastorate December 31, in the year 1893.

During his pastorate seventy-nine members by baptism or letter were added to the Church.

The years 1882–83 formed a critical period in the history of this Church.

It was the culminating period in a distressing series of financial disasters and spiritual barrenness.

It was the "Harvest Home," when were garnered the Dead Sea fruits of unwise and, as the result proved, almost ruinous business mismanagement.

Many who had been active and prominent in the affairs of the Church were gone.

Some were alienated, some driven out by a spirit of intolerance, some were dead, some removed to other places.

A decade of business blunders and mistakes of management had given birth to unchristian feelings and harsh recrimination, so that the year of our Lord 1882 found but a few left who were willing to stand by the fortunes of this venerable church, when the storm-waves were beating high upon her walls and undermining her foundations.

It was, indeed, a time of peril which made all those who loved the church, for herself, her history and her mission, realize that there was need of all being done that could be done by all who still clung to the cause, and were willing to go on, hoping and trusting that in His own time and way God would raise up instrumentalities for the care and perpetuation of this, His Zion.

So serious was the condition in the years 1881 and 1882, that it was with great difficulty the Treasurer could raise the paltry, weekly stipend of ten dollars, then the pay received by the Rev. Mr. Guiscard, the then Pastor, while at the same time the meeting house, the Parsonage and the grounds around them were steadily falling into dilapidation and decay; and, still worse, the time when the interest upon the Mortgage debt of the Church, if not the debt itself, would have to be met, and with absolutely no provision being made or thought possible to be made to meet either.

It is not a matter of wonder that in such circumstances, a proposition was seriously made by a trustee, at a meeting of the Board, that the Meeting House and other property of the Church covered by the Mortgages (which were held by Warren Ackerman, Esquire, who had generously forborne the interest thereon for five years), should be abandoned, and the property surrendered.

As the Mortgages covered everything belonging to the Church which could be Mortgaged, real and personal, even down to the Communion Service, such abandonment could not be permitted.

This brief sketch outlines the perilous conditions which existed in the years 1881-2; the inheritance from former years of mistakes and mismanagement.

Every one, or nearly every one, felt that it was quite time to call upon a leader who could devote zeal with knowledge, experience and business ability to the work of rescue and relief—a man who would be a brave and skilful Captain, to lead the "forlorn hope," and save the dear old church from utter annihilation.

On the twenty-seventh day of November, 1882, by a unanimous vote, the church extended a call to become its Pastor, to the Rev. James H. Parks, and on the Eighth day of December, next thereafter, at a special Parish Meeting called to consider the subject, the call so made by the church, was cordially and with practical unanimity endorsed by the Parish, there being only three dissenting votes.

After consultation with the trustees, and after receiving from each member of the Board his personal assurance that he would stand by, help, aid and assist, with Prayers and work, and with a full knowledge of the direful condition, spiritual and financial, which surrounded the task before him, the Reverend James H. Parks accepted the call which he had received, and entered upon the arduous work before him, on the second week of January, 1883.

Of a truth, the labor was great, but seemed to be to the new pastor a labor of love as well, and success seemed to crown his efforts at the very beginning.

His organizing talent and executive ability, reinforced by remarkable energy, inspired all around him with kindred vitality and strength of purpose. Where fear and despair had so lately held their paralyzing sway, faith re-asserted herself. Hope arose to newness of life, courage once more filled and fired all hearts; and very soon under their wise and careful leader, every one was a willing, cheerful co-worker for the redemption of the old church from her bondage of debt.

Methods were adopted to meet the accruing interest on the mortgage debt, provision was made for the current expenses of the Church, and a brave and successful attack was planned and carried into effect too for the reduction of the principal of the mortgage debt.

REV. J. H. PARKS, D.D.

Although those were days of serious thought and severe and incessant toil, they were also times of great enjoyment. Peace reigned in our councils, and harmony of purpose and action wrought their natural work. Pastor and people were united.

They could see that, with God's blessing, they were gaining ground and could even anticipate the time when the last fetter of debt should be knocked off and the Scotch Plains Baptist Church should be again, what for more than a Century she had been, dedicated to the Lord's service, free and clear of all debt.

Among the means to this glorious end introduced by the new Pastor, one ought not to pass unmentioned in the annals of those days of trial and triumph, viz. : The Ladies' Circle.

The New Pastor had brought with him an helpmeet, invaluable to himself and to the Church, and when upon the Organization of "THE LADIES' CIRCLE," Mrs. Parks became its President, with Mrs. Huldah D. Cleaver as Vice President, Miss Mary Dunn, Treasurer, Miss Hannah Hayes, Secretary, and a Board of Managers, there came into life one of the most, if not the most potent factors for the success of the work in hand.

Under the wise and skilful guidance of their beloved President, who worked with her head, her heart, and her hands, the ladies of the Church, without regard to age, rallied with an ardor that shed new lustre upon the sex, and worked with the utmost zeal and untiring energy. Indeed more money was raised through this splendid band of women, than through any other one agency then in operation.

Thus, under the judicious Management of Doctor Parks, the work of getting the Church upon solid ground went bravely and successfully on.

Doctor Parks had some heroic co-workers in those days, foremost among whom was Doctor F. W. Westcott.

It may be permitted to mention here some incidents of how they then worked. The Furnace underneath the Church was so out of Order (and to get a new one was impossible) that the Auditorium could only be warmed for Sunday Service by having someone sit up all the night before with the furnace and coax it along.

Doctors Parks and Westcott were the men for the Emergency. They did it alternately, and thus the old furnace was forced to do duty until a new one could be bought.

When the Ladies' Circle gave Entertainments at which oysters were served, it was a sight well worth the seeing, and not easily to be forgotten by those who understood all that it meant, to see these two Doctors, Parks and Westcott, standing with coats off, and sleeves rolled up, opening the rough-coated bivalves, for the guests at the festivals.

It was a homely but needed work. They did it well. They honored the work. The work honored them. They were working for the Master's Cause, and their work met His approval, and was crowned with success.

Space does not permit the narration of other incidents to illustrate the character and toilsomeness of the services and sacrifices made by the Men and Women, and Children also, of the Parish in that period of Supreme Struggle. Suffice it to say: All were animated by the high and holy resolve to save the old Church, and their resolve was chrystalized into action.

The Lord blessed their efforts, and from the nettle of seeming Ruin, they plucked the fragrant flower of Victory.

Pastor and People were of one mind, enthusiastic and happy.

They saw the dark and ominous cloud, which had hovered so low and so long, over them passing away, and the dawn of a better and brighter day was beginning to purple the east.

Church and Parish were laboring as a unit. Faith and Good works blended in one harmonious impulse, and under the sway of such motors, all were content to work on assured of the blessing of the Most High. During this time the interest was paid and $2,000 on mortgage debt. Thus it was and thus continued the surroundings of the Church, when in the year 1888, Matthias Frazee Lee, an old member of the church died, and by his will, made her the residuary legatee of an estate estimated to be worth One hundred and fifty thousand Dollars ($150,000) or more.

This will was drawn up by Mr. Lee's legal adviser, and was made and executed absolutely without the knowledge of the church or any of its members, except only the testator himself.

As is usual in such cases, the dead man's will and wishes in regard to the disposition of his property were not respected.

He was a bachelor. He had no one dependent upon him. He was under no obligation to any of his relatives.

His next of kin were two uncles, both older than himself, both comfortably well off as to "this world's gear." One of them was a member of this church, the other belonged to the Presbyterian Church of Westfield, New Jersey.

These two men set on foot legal proceedings to nullify the last will and testament of their nephew, who had lived all his life near neighbor to them, and whom they knew to be a man of far more than ordinary mind and capacity for business.

It was evident, as the case developed, that the uncles were mere "figureheads" in the contest.

That they had permitted themselves to be used by others who were not next of kin to the Testator.

These people, most of whom were cousins to Mr. Lee, many of whom had shared his bounty during his lifetime—these instigators of the attack upon the will of Mr. Lee made their appearance at the Court. (The old men whose names were used as nominal contestants did not appear), and did their utmost to cover with shame and obloquy the life, career and memory of the man whose money they sought to grasp against his wish and will, solemnly expressed.

As the real parties to this shameful scheme, they dragged the vicinity for willing and unwilling witnesses—many of whom were debtors to Mr. Lee—they themselves; some of them became witnesses, and in their own interest swore down the dead man's character, his wishes and his will.

The outcome was that the church became weary of the long and expensive contest against avarice; a compromise was made, and they who had fought so viciously for their kinsman's money, which

SOME MEMBERS OF THE LADIES CIRCLE.

they knew he intended they should not have, carried off the major part of the estate. Let us not envy them all the pleasure they can derive from wealth thus obtained.

The small portion of the original estate which finally came to the church, enabled the Trustees to obey the first condition of the legacy, by paying the debt of the church. The balance of the fund is held by the terms of the Will "to be used by said Church in spreading the Gospel."

Another event which marked the Pastorate of Doctor Parks, and seemed to characterize it as the Era of Legacies, was that of the death of James C. Lyon, (which took place July 7, 1890), another former member of the church having departed this life, made the church the residuary legatee under his last Will. Happily this gift came unattended by the disagreeable and exasperating displays of greed which marked the Lee bequest; and so in due season, and in conformity with the will of the testator, his executor, William C. Stanbery, Esquire, turned over to the church the residue of the Estate valued at about Ten thousand Dollars ($10,000). This legacy came as a free gift untrammelled by any restrictions or limitations.

Let the memory of Lee and Lyon ever be kept freshly and lovingly in the minds of the sons and daughters of our old Zion. A beautiful memorial tablet has been erected conspicuously upon the church building to each of those benefactors of the church.

The first decade of Doctor Parks' Pastorate was, simply, a struggle for life.

The Old Ship which for more than a century had sailed upon her course safely and steadily bearing the "glad tidings" the Gospel of Love and Salvation, was now tempest tossed—storm beaten —well nigh wrecked. Self preservation, the first law of nature, demanded that every energy of Captain, Officers and Crew, should be directed to saving the ship, well knowing, as they did, that unless the ship were saved from wreck, her long and noble voyage, already sailed, would end disastrously and forever.

If therefore it should appear to the reader of this review of Doctor Park's Pastorate, that too much time and labor were devoted to the worldly or financial interests of the Church, and too little to her spiritual growth ; it is felt that the criticism must be toned down and softened by the recollection of the stern and unrelenting necessities which threatened the very existence of the Church.

But the spiritual things—the preaching and prayer services were never at anytime neglected or intermitted.

The Christian Graces were reared and fortified in the school of severe practical training and alert watchfulness. It was a discipline of realities in which Faith and Good Works so constantly met and mingled, that old-time Christians were strengthened and renewed, while the Novitiates felt their hearts warmed, and under the inspiration of the constant struggle for the cause, were built up and made to "quit themselves like men."

The latter years of Doctor Parks' Pastorate were marked by a quiet and gradual growth in the Church, and when he decided to resign the charge he so faithfully had kept for eleven years, his resignation was accepted by Church and Parish with unaffected and universal regret.

REV. JAMES S. BRAKER.

He carried with him into his retirement, the esteem and respect of the community, and the sincere love of his Parishioners and Church Members.

He is now living in his own home, opposite the scene of his recent labors; and may the Lord bless and keep him and his estimable wife for years yet to come.

The present Pastor of the church is Rev. J. S. Braker. He was born in Camden, N. J., in 1863, and was educated at Bucknell University and Crozer Theological Seminary. He has held pastorates at Passayunk Baptist Church and at Temple Baptist Church, Philadelphia, Pa. He accepted the call of this church in April, 1894. His pastorate is yet too young to record results—But he has the hearty co-operation of the church. He has baptised a number into its fellowship, and all hope he may be successful in accomplishing the will of the God of the church.

Thus Jehovah has always provided leaders for His people, who have broken to them the bread of life, and conducted them amid the intricacies of the way heavenward.

LICENTIATES.

Lay preaching was at least tacitly authorized as long ago as 1791 when it was "voted that the deacons exercise their gifts in case of disappointment by the minister." The minutes, also record instances in which persons asked for license to preach the gospel, and after the church "had investigated and inquired into their fitness," they were advised that "they would be more useful in some other department of the Lord's vineyard."

The following persons, however, were licensed by vote of the church.

Henry Crosley, one of the original members, was licensed about the year 1750, and was ordained at Schooley's Mountain in 1753.

David Sutton was baptised by Rev. Mr. Miller, soon after the church was constituted, and was licensed in 1758 and ordained in 1761.

John Sutton, who was a brother of David, was baptised, licensed and ordained at the same time his brother was, and became an eminently useful Minister of the Gospel.

James Manning, D. D., was baptised by Rev. Mr. Miller, licensed and ordained at Scotch Plains. Elsewhere his great usefulness and the eminence he attained in the Denomination, have been recorded.

Daniel Dane was baptised in August, 1771, and licensed to preach the gospel in 1773.

Jacob F. Randolph was baptised by Rev. Mr. Van Horn in 1786 and licensed in 1791. He had previously exercised his talents in the occasional absence of the Pastor. He was ordained at Mount Bethel in the same year, and afterward served as Pastor at Samptown; and when the Plainfield First Baptist Church was organized in 1818 he became their Pastor. He was devotedly pious, ardently zealous, and possessed a peculiar sweetness of disposition. He was Pastor at Plainfield about ten years, and died in the triumphs of the Christian faith.

Marmaduke Earl who was a member of the Reformed Dutch Church and graduate of Columbia College, became a baptist in 1789. He united with this Church in 1790 and was licensed to preach in 1791. He was Pastor for several years at Oyster Bay, L. I.

Henry Ball, son of Deacon Aaron Ball, was licensed to preach in 1805. He labored twenty-seven years at Brookfield, N. Y., and afterward was useful at Greenville, Factoryville and Middletown, N. Y. At the latter place he was instrumental in organizing a Baptist Church, which has since become a strong people.

Obediah B. Brown of Newark, came to Scotch Plains, to study under direction of Rev. Mr. Van Horn. He was licensed January 1, 1806. Soon after, he accompanied Deacon Ezra Darby, M. C., to Washington, D. C., and became Pastor of a church in that City.

Hervey Ball, nephew of Henry Ball, was graduated at Columbian College, Washington, D.C., and was soon after licensed to preach. His life was spent chiefly in teaching.

Elias Frost was licensed in 1830 and removed to Hamburg, Sussex Co., N. J.

These are all whom the minutes record as having received license directly from this church; though others who have been members with us, and removed to sister churches, have received license from the respective churches to which they went.

DEACONS.

It should be said here, that when the church was organized, officers were elected who are not usually recognized by Baptist churches. They were called Ruling Elders, and seem to have constituted an Advisory Board with the Pastor. The office continued for about forty years, and was then quietly allowed to drop out of sight. Those who occupied this position were William Darby, Recompense Stanbery, Peter Wilcox, John Stites, Samuel Drake, Samuel Doty, John Blackford and Joseph Manning.

Recompense Stanbery and William Darby were the first deacons. They were elected at the first business meeting of the church, October 14, 1747. They were chosen to the double office of Deacon and Ruling Elder. They served faithfully and well until their death. Joseph Allen was elected April 6, 1748, and retained the office until his death in 1797.

Gabriel Ogden and Samuel Brooks were elected in July, 1765. Deacon Ogden was dismissed upon his removal to Sussex Co., and Deacon Brooks died March 24, 1788.

Joseph F. Randolph was elected July 30, 1777, and died in 1782.

David Morris was elected in October, 1777, and served until he removed to Kentucky in 1788.

Daniel Drake was a deacon and died October 1, 1777.

Nathaniel Drake was a younger brother of Daniel, and became a deacon and discharged his duties until his death in 1801.

Noah Clark was chosen a deacon and served until his death in 1801, a period of about ten years.

Benjamin Blackford was elected in 1791, and served until his removal to Samptown at the organization of that church.

Melvin Parse was appointed to succeed Deacon Blackford, and served thirty-four years until the time of his death in 1827.

Aaron Ball was chosen in 1793, and continued in office more than forty-eight years.

John B. Osborn and Ezra Darby were elected February 13, 1802. Deacon Osborn served until his death. Deacon Darby was chosen to represent the State in the Congress of the United States in 1804. While performing his duties at the Capitol, he was suddenly removed by death, January 28, 1808. He was buried in the Congressional Cemetery which is a beautiful spot situated about two miles from the Capitol, on the banks of the "East Branch" of the Potomac River. His name is number two in the list of interments. His tomb is situated in the North East corner of the cemetery on a gentle mound, overlooking the peaceful valley of the "Eastern Branch," and the picturesque hills of Maryland beyond. The inscription on the tomb is simply "In memory of Ezra Darby, born at Scotch Plains, New Jersey. Member of Congress from that State. Died in this City, January 28, 1808. In the 39th year of his age. A Patriot. A Philanthropist. A Christian."

James Brown was elected to fill Deacon Darby's place in 1809. He died June 5, 1811.

Henry Hetfield was appointed in 1828, and served about sixteen years, when he removed his church relationship to Brooklyn, N. Y., and afterwards to Somerville, N. J. He was re-elected when he returned, and served until the Master called him home.

Jonathan Osborn was chosen on 27th of July, 1830, and served until 1842, when he removed to the State of New York.

Dr. Corra Osborn, Alexander Wilson, William Hand, Maxwell Frazee, Corra O. Meeker and James

Pugsley were all elected between 1841 and 1844, and filled the office well and faithfully. Randolph G. Silvers was also an efficient deacon. Jared S. Stout and L. H. K. Smalley have also served the church honorably and satisfactorily until they were called up higher.

During the last fifteen years or more, William Archbold, David Hand, Dr. J. A. Coles and Thomas Mead have consecratedly and devoutly occupied the office. Deacon Mead removed to Spring Valley, N. Y., last year, and resigned his position.

CLERKS.

As appears by the minutes, those who have performed the duties of clerk, have been Recompense Stanbery, Ichabod Valentine, Jr., David Morris, Robert F. Randolph, Aaron Ball, Ezra Darby, Jonathan Hand Osborn, Jonathan Osborn, Jr., Alexander Wilson, C. O. Meeker, Thomas Ward, O. M. Putnam, L. H. K. Smalley, Thomas Cleaver, R. C. Treadwell and George Dunn.

Bro. Dunn is now acting in that capacity. Thus the church has been fully officered during all the years of its existence. Even during the dark times of the Revolutionary Struggle, while the minutes of that period are scant and unsatisfactory, and the business meetings irregular, yet the church maintained its existence, and kept the banner of the cross in sight.

MISCELLANEOUS.

The church has always defended Baptist principles: among these, soul liberty, or rights of conscience, by which our fathers understood that every one has a right to think and believe without dictation from any earthly power, being responsible to God only. To worship God according to the dictates of his own conscience. A century and a half ago this principle was not so generally endorsed by other denominations as it is now, but it has always been the teaching of Baptists.

When the province of New Jersey was ceded to Lord Berkley and Sir George Cartaret, by the Duke of York, in 1664, religious freedom was guaranteed in the charter thus: "No person at any time shall be anyways molested, punished, disquieted, or called in question for any difference of opinion or practice in matters of religious concernment." This was the broad teaching which our fathers loved, but it was not always conformed to by paedobaptists of this and neighboring provinces.

In 1775 Baptists as well as others, were required to pay a rate ministerial tax for the support of Presbyterian and Congregational clergymen, in some of the provinces. Our fathers felt themselves wronged, aggrieved and persecuted by this requirement. When knowledge of the fact came to the ears of this church, on the first of February, 1775, they appointed one Mr. Smith, to go to England to represent and defend these persecuted brethren. The church paid the expenses of Mr. Smith upon this mission.

Dr. Manning, and Dr. Stennett, who was known personally to George III, succeeded in getting the ear of the King. The consequence was that His Majesty "disallowed and rejected" all acts of oppression of Baptists: and thus one of the first victories of soul liberty secured on this continent was gained by the co-operation of this church, and the payment of the expenses of one of its members, as one of a committee upon this business.

The church has always been a Strict Communion church. It has always believed and taught that they only were entitled to the privilege of the Lord's table, who had been immersed on profession of faith, and were living upright and consistent lives. Our fathers were uncompromising in their tenacious adherence to this principle. Not only would they refuse to commune with an unbaptised person, but the minutes record instances in which their own members were "Set by," and refused the Lord's Supper until they had acknowledged some fault, or repented of some sin, or indiscretion of which they had been guilty. No officer of this church would ever have been elected, or held his position long, if he had been at all wavering or uncertain upon the communion question. So, too, of the doctrines of the church. They have always been unequivocally stated and implicitly believed. The Bible has ever been our only rule of faith and practice. While the church adopted the Philadelphia Confession of Faith, yet it has never conformed to any creed as such, but always tried every summary of doctrine, by the word of God and endorsed that which would bear the test of its teachings. We have reason to rejoice that our fathers laid the foundations of our Zion deep and strong, and that hitherto the superstructure has been erected upon that foundation.

The church has been pecuniarily self-sustaining from its organization. It has never received any help or assistance from Home Mission Society, State Convention, nor any other benevolent organization of our denomination; while it has always counted it a privilege to contribute to the needs of others; not to the extent of our ability, perhaps, but always in some degree.

The church has been at peace with itself from the beginning. No serious inharmony nor dissension has ever prevailed, and we have never had occasion to call a council of the denomination to settle disputes. To the Great Head in Zion be the praise and not to us. We are doubtless as heady and strong willed as any in the Lord's great family, but His moulding and modifying hand has been upon us from the beginning even until now.

The church has never been numerically large. Though about one thousand persons have been baptised since the organization, yet the membership at any one time has never been large. The reason for this is apparent. We are geographically located away from the railroad and are surrounded with Baptist churches. Besides this there are few manufacturing interests in our immediate vicinity. For this reason young persons who have been converted and united with the church have only remained until they could find employment elsewhere. Hence the church has always been a feeder to other churches. Young men and women have been trained in church work here, and then have gone to enrich the working force of other churches, while few have located permanently with us. We count it a privilege to have thus contributed to the greater efficiency of neighboring organizations through all these past years, and regard it a success if we have maintained a creditable average membership.

The female membership has been an important factor in the success of every church enterprise. The records show that while women have never been entrusted with any official church position, yet the affectionately devoted lives, and hearty co-operation with every good word and work, of many of them, has endeared them to the church and made their memory hallowed when they have passed away. Indeed, many a wisely planned scheme for church enlargement and progress would have failed but for the prayers, self-sacrificing identification, deft fingers and determined application of sisters of the church, who regarded no effort too great to make, for the cause so dear to their hearts. The Ladies' Circle in the time of the church's greatest financial need helped to carry the burden for years, and assisted in raising both the principal and interest of the mortgage debt. All honor to the consecrated women who were surely related to the Marys of old, who were last at the cross and first at the sepulchre of our risen Lord.

The Sabbath School was organized during the pastorate of Rev. John Rogers, in the year 1829, just sixty-eight years ago. Catechetical and Bible class instruction, however, was given by the Pastors of the church before that time. The East New Jersey Baptist Sunday School Convention was not organized until 1852, and our Sunday School immediately united with it. Its second session was held with this church and school in 1853. It is impossible to collate the names of all who have served as Superintendents, but the following named are distinctly remembered by some of the oldest living members of the church: Deacon Henry Hetfield, for twenty-five years, Thomas Ward, Thomas Cleaver, James E. Pugsley, Randolph Silvers, Anson Grant, H. E. Need-

SOME OF THE DEACONS.

ham, Charles A. Smith, L. H. K. Smalley, David
Hand, R. C. Treadwell, George Colgate and George
E. Hall. Bro. Hall is in charge of the school at
this time, and is efficiently promoting its interests.
He is also President of the East N. J. Baptist S.
S. Convention. All of these officers have been
among the most public spirited, self sacrificing
and consecrated members of the church. There
has always been a corps of teachers too, of both
sexes, who have labored in this nursery of Zion,
and God has not left them destitute of evidence of
His approval.

It is undoubtedly a historical fact, that among
the great army of Sunday School workers in our
State, it may be declared that this or that man
was born into the Kingdom of God by the influence of the Scotch Plains Baptist Sunday School.

The church has had thirteen regular Pastors, of
whom four are yet living, viz.: Rev. J. F. Brown,
D.D., Rev. J. C. Buchanan, D.D., Rev. J. H.
Parks, D.D. and Rev. J. S. Braker, the present
Pastor. Two of these Pastors were ordained here,
viz.: Benjamin Miller and Joseph C. Buchanan,
and two are buried here, viz.: Rev. Benj. Miller
and Rev. Joshua E. Rue. The longest term of
office continued thirty-four years, and the shortest
twenty months. The average is more than twelve
years.

DESCENDANTS OF ORIGINAL FAMILIES.

Of course the constituent members of the church
have long since gone to their final home and their
reward, but some of their descendants are still
residents of our town.

Recompense Stanbery, one of the constituent members and deacons, had children, among whom were Recompense Stanbery, born September 23, 1758. He also was identified with the church. Nine children were the result of his marriage, of whom but one remains, William C. Stanbery, who is an honored and respected member of our community.

Rev. Benjamin Miller left one son, who lived in the homestead, the farm now occupied by our honored townsman, A. D. Shepard. He had several children. Aaron Drake married one of the granddaughters. Two of his children, Miss Sarah Drake and Miss Louise Barr, are now identified with us and are the only members of the church who are direct descendants of the first pastor.

John Darby, one of the early members, married Nancy Stanbery. He had several children. Levi, Aaron, John, Joseph, Recompense, William, Katie and Margaret. William H. Cleaver married Margaret, and Judge James D. Cleaver, one of the sons of this union, is a member of our Board of Trustees. He was President of the Board in 1847, and is again President this present year, 1897. Levi Darby, who is yet with us, is a son of Aaron Darby. Albert B. Darby, now of Plainfield, is a son of Joseph, who was a member and trustee of this church fifty years ago, and his widow is still a member of this church.

Benjamin Stites, whose name often appears in the old records, had three sons—Henry, Foster and Benjamin. Mrs. James D. Cleaver who died only two years ago, the wife of Judge Cleaver, was the daughter of Benjamin. Henry Stites, who passed away in 1894, was the son of Foster,

Mrs. Gershom Little, who now resides in our community is the daughter of Henry.

James Coles came into this community in the last century. One of his sons was Dennis Coles, who was the father of our lamented fellow member, Dr. Abraham Coles, L.L.D., and of Mrs. Susan Stout. He was the grandfather of Dr. J. Ackerman Coles and his sister Emily who are still in church relationship with us. Dennis Crane, another grandson, is also a member of the church.

Dr. Corra Osborn was a deacon of the church and a prominent and influential member. He left several children. one of whom married Samuel Hayes. She was an active and useful member until 1892 when she died, leaving three daughters, Mary, Hannah and Lydia, who are still efficient workers with us.

There are other representatives of the old members living, some still in our community, and others in other parts of the Lord's heritage.

These all cherish a commendable and fervent love for the old church home. They rejoice in every success which attends the labors of those who are working in the old vineyard; and believe that God has blessed every scripturally inspired effort which has been made by His people in all the eventful years of its history.

The Present Officers of the Church are

      Rev. J. S. Braker, Pastor.
      William Archbold, Deacon.
      Dr. J. A. Coles,   "
      David Hand,   "
      George L. Dunn, Church Clerk.
      George E. Hall, Treasurer.

TRUSTEES.

CONCLUSION.

The history of one hundred and fifty years is completed. While the workers of other years have passed away, God has raised up others in their place, for "while the laborers cease the work goes on."

The fidelity and constancy of our forefathers amid difficulties and discouragements is an example to us which we may well emulate. Their work is ended. Their remains repose in this silent cemetery until the summons of the Great King in the last great day.—Here they saw the cross and endured the toil, and here they will see the King in His beauty. Their work is transferred to us. It is a glorious inheritance. It ought to arouse our zeal and our grandest efforts for the honor of the Master. May the church continue until Christ's second appearing, and may we contribute our share to the accomplishment of the purposes of the great Head in Zion.

THE TRUSTEES — 1897.

THE OLD MEETING HOUSE

AT

SCOTCH PLAINS,

A Mid-Summers Sabbath in, and about it,

FIFTY YEARS AND MORE AGO.

———

BY JAMES D. CLEAVER.

Not many will come up to our Sesqui Centennial Anniversary, who were here at the date of this sketch which is Ante-Centennial.

Most of them have gone on to the "undiscovered country from whose bourne no traveller returns." Many of them are quietly resting in the Old Burying Ground, their mortal remains lying around those of the Reverend Benjamin Miller, the first and beloved pastor of the church in the bivouac of death, awaiting the reveille, which on the morning of the Resurrection, shall call them from their slumber to the realities of that day.

Of the remaining few, the writer is one. He writes from Memory, and hopes to be substantially correct in what he states.

The day was a Sabbath; indeed. The sun rose brightly, and ushered in a day of rest for the quiet old village and the neighboring farms. Over all reigned an air of peaceful contentment which gave promise of a day full of worshipful experience, which should hallow the hours with heavenly joy and blessing, while it's duties and services should comfort and strengthen all who should share in it's Mission of Love to God and Man.

Under the sway of such influences it was easy to say with Coleridge:

"He prayeth well, who loveth well
"Both Man, and Beast and Bird;
"He prayeth best, who loveth best
"All things, both great and small;
"For the dear God, who loveth us,
"He made and loveth all."

The Old Meeting House, which was of frame and covered roof and sides with shingles, painted white, without porch or spire, or any architectural ornament, stood at quite a distance from the road (now Park Avenue).

It was flanked on the northwest and on the rear by the Burying Ground. On the southeast was "The Green," reaching eastwardly, to the School House which then stood on the line of the side walk, nearly where the present church building stands.

"The Green" or Lawn had upon it a grove of fine trees, oaks and hickories.

It was the play ground for the school children; it was the place where the soldiers of the early days, met, "horse and foot," on "training days," and were drilled in their manual.

"The Green," was, also, where the annual "Town Meetings" were held, and where the early politicians displayed their eloquence and their skill in guiding the Ship of State.

"The Green," was not fenced on the front or road side, but was open to all:—It has disappeared now, with the Old Meeting House, and the Old School House which then stood on its southeasterly and northwesterly corners as sentinels of religion and education. The Lawn now extending along Park Avenue northwesterly from the present church building marks the location of the old "Green."

On such a Sabbath as I am speaking of "The Green" was the drawing room of the parish, where ante-sermon receptions were held.

Without, as within, the Old Meeting House was devoid of ornament or architectural pretension. It's two doors of entrance, each opening into one of the two aisles within, were approached by stone stoops, three steps high, no porches or railings protected them.

There were two rows of square windows, one above the other, on the sides, and a long narrow window, on either side of the Pulpit, in the rear wall.

No shutters, or shades or blinds were there to shut out the sun.

The "dim religious light" now so great a desideratum in modern sanctuaries, was an unknown quantity there.

Galleries extended around the sides and front of the auditorium.

These were terraced, and constituted the Sunday School room of those days.

They also, usually, accommodated the flotsam and jetsam of the parish with sittings, free of charge.

The Sunday School was primitive and unpretending.

The teachers did not "know it all," and prudently confined themselves to the printed questions and answers contained in the lesson books.

The library was not extensive or various.

The books were as dry as they were few; the Librarian went from class to class with his stock of books displayed on a board shelf which he carried in front of him, and the scholars accepted with meek resignation the book given them; they had no choice in those days; nor did it take a faithful reader long to "go through" the entire list, so that being deprived of "a choice" mattered but little.

No stage then brought the children to Sunday School.

If their parents thought the children were well, the children came—having nothing to do with the business, except to obey, and attend.

Sunday School Excursions had not invaded this secluded spot —as to Picnics—well, there were times when on the glorious fourth of July, the Sunday School was assembled on " the Green," and the youthful hearts fired with patriotism by weak rhetoric and weaker lemonade.—Excuse the digression.

Let us return to the Meeting House. Within, the floor space was divided by the two aisles leading from the doors of entrance, into three parcels of pews, two wall slips and the central body, the pews of which reached half way from aisle to aisle.

THE BUILDING IN THE BACKGROUND IS THE OLD CHURCH AS IT STOOD FROM 1819 TO 1870.

THE OLD
SCHOOL HOUSE
ERECTED A.D.
1786

The pews were straight up and down, made of very hard boards and so high of backs and seats that a boy of fourteen could, with difficulty, "see out" while he was standing, or "touch bottom" when sitting down.

The floors were uncarpeted, save on some extraordinary occasion, when they were ornamented with a top-dressing of "Rockaway sand." The house was warmed in the winter, at least two corners of it were, by two immense stoves known as the "ten-plate" variety. These were fired with great hickory and oak billets, and, when in full blast, made their immediate vicinity unbearably hot, while at the other end of the room, the mercury was down to zero. Still it is likely that the temperature, had it been fairly averaged, would have marked about "temperate." The house was lighted! by a system of tallow candles, held in tin holders, at the end of crooked wires, attached to the square wooden pillars which supported the galleries.

The naps of the bad boys and girls who slept in "meetin' time," were disturbed at stated intervals, by the Sexton, who went around the aisles, with heavy tread and creaking shoes, Snuffers in hand, to snuff the candles, and make darkness visible.

The prominent feature of the "Interior" was, however, the Pulpit. From it came the "bread of life," as it was broken by the Pastor. From it issued "in tones of love or warning fear," instruction, appeal, admonition, reproof, rebuke, threatening. It was the central point and fountain for the people, and its influence for good in the community was recognized and gratefully acknowledged.

The Pulpit was located between the long windows in the rear wall, and was suspended about mid-way between the floor and the ceiling, so as to be plainly visible from the remotest part of the room. It was reached by a long winding stairway, and a cushioned seat afforded room for two or three people.

The preachers of those days seemed to prefer an elevated place from which to reach their hearers.

There was no "sounding board" overhead. Underneath the Pulpit was a recess which contained the book-case (about the size of an ordinary wardrobe), holding the Library of the Sunday School. In front of the recess were four large rush bottomed arm chairs, which at Communion and other important occasions contained the four Deacons; who to us boys, were awful in their solemn dignity.

Thus was the Old Meeting House the one that had arisen from the ashes of its predecessor.

No spire or belfry rose above its roof, and no "church-going bell" rang out over the Plains to ummon the worshippers to the Sanctuary.

Nevertheless, they came. Let me recall some of them as they came up from their homes that day, to join in their Sabbath day's worship.

There came the brothers, Silas and Mulford Cole, from their brook farm—they came out to the Plainfield road, now Front street.

They then joined the sisters Jemima and Emmeline Shotwell, who came from their father's house on the hill just beyond.

From the "Short Hills," near Netherwood and the "Terrill Road," there are coming Corra O. Meeker and Deacon William Hand, Grandfather of our present Deacon David Hand, and with them come the Lees, the Garthwaites, the Hetfields, the Dolbiers, the Lines, the Crisps and "Aunt Betsy Terrill," the last representative of the family which gave its name to that road.

As these come out on the Plainfield Road, they are joined, or followed by "Aunt Katie Cole," and the families of Melvin Parse, Amos Osborn, Jonathan Hand Osborn, Joseph Bradford, Deacon Henry Hetfield, Vincent L. Frazee, William H. Cleaver, Noah and Cooper Parse, Jotham D. Frazee, "Aunt Phebe Darby," widow of Ezra Darby, formerly Member of Congress; the families of Samuel Vermeule, Gideon Allen, the Moffetts, Simeon V. and Amos, Joseph M. Osborn, afterward Sheriff of Union County, Jonathan Osborn, Jr., formerly Sheriff of Essex County and Thomas J. Barr, then the Keeper of the Old Tavern. N. B. It was not thought disreputable in those good old days for a hotel keeper to attend church.

Going over a point further east to "The Darby Road," now Park ave., there came up by that way to our church, the Lamberts, the Sisters Hetfield, Deacon James E. Pugsley and family, also the families of Aaron and Levi Darby, the Platts, John Darby and Benjamin S. Hetfield.

Another point eastward brings us over to the Westfield road, and up from that old village, and beyond, we have coming as worshippers at our altar the widow of Thomas Clark with her sons, the families of Jacob Cole, brother to Silas above named, Doctor Corra Osborn, M.D., father of the late Mrs. Samuel Hays; she was one of the true and tried friends of the church in the years of peril and poverty. With them came Major Aaron

Ball, who for years acted as Precentor, and led the congregational singing. After these came John B. Osborn, surnamed "the little," the Adair brothers, Shuttleworth and George W.; then the families of William Osborn, and of Deacons John and Jonathan Osborne, and with them the Wilcox and Marsh, and Ryno families; coming 'round the corner, known as "Pfaff's," these were joined by the households of Andrew Schuyler, Oliver Hand, surnamed "the Lawyer," Abraham Nelson, "Aunt Rachel Darby," Aaron Drake, Alexander Wilson, a scholarly man, who often expounded the Scriptures, at the evening meetings in the upper room of the Old School House, John W. Osborn and Judge Corey.

Looking, now, further toward the north, we may see another contingent of our friends, coming in by the Springfield road—now Mountain Avenue. From the Branch Mills neighborhood come the families of William Darby, William Richards, Carlisle and Erastus Miller, James Roll and William H. Darby.

Coming hitherward, these are re-inforced by the families of James Coles and his father, Esquire Dennis Coles, who was the father of the late Doctor Abraham Coles, M. D., and Grandfather of our present Deacon, Doctor Jonathan Ackerman Coles, M. D., and these were joined by Captain William Abel and Robert Walpole with their folk.

From Feltville, or as the locality was known in the early days, "the Old Powder Mill," where in Revolutionary days, the Continental Army, more especially "the Jersey Blues," drew largely their supply of powder, then manufactured up in that secluded nook—from their mountain farm up there, came Thomas and William Ward, two stalwart brothers.

Still further around toward the north west, down by the New Providence Road, sometimes called "The Turkey Road," we may see coming down to join the Congregation, the Townleys and Deacon Maxwell Frazee, with his large family, while from the Washington Valley and the Mount Bethel way, the procession is supplemented by the families of James C. Lyon, the Archibalds, of whom I believe our worthy Deacon, William Archibald and his brother John, are now the only representatives left, Lyman Spencer and Nathaniel Drake, Jr.; and coming down the eastern slope of the mountain these were joined by the families of Amos Cole, Nathaniel Drake, Isaac Drake, Joseph S. Darby and Gauin McCoy, David Frazee and John Mooney, while on the Plains, east of Green Brook, the line was increased by the households of Col. Stanbery, Matthew S. Dunn, "Aunt Sally Stites" and Aaron B. Allen. Thus they came, from every point of the compass, on foot, on horseback, in comfortable wagons and in covered carriages.

As they reached "the Green," and cared for their teams, they began at once the first duty and pleasure of the hour, that of the social nature.

In that place and hour there were no class distinction: all met on a common plane. No rich, no poor, no high, no low. All were friends and neighbors, and most of them were of kin to each other.

As group after group arrived, and joined those already there, the welcomes went around with sincerest feeling. The glances of recognition, the smile of pleasure at meeting, gave wealth of honest reality to the voices which spake, and to the hearty hand shaking which emphasized the greetings given by all to all.

Those present exchanged their genuine and unaffected salutations, and the absent ones were all enquired after.

All were not Church members, all were not professing Christians; but all who came there were such as revered the Most High, honored His Religion, and His Sabbath, and respected the services of the hour.

The day was a perfect one, an ideal Sabbath. The sun had now risen high overhead, and was giving warmth, and life, and light and color to all created things animate and inanimate. On the northwest, the sky-line was shown by the waves of the range of hills which marked the boundary of the plain in that direction, and were clad in all the pomp of their green and misty purple foliage.

The Old Mill which stood hard by, had ceased its work-a-day clatter, the ponderous mill-stones hung quietly upon their spindles, the whir of the iron cogs in the big wheel-pit was hushed, and the great master wheel, suspended on its mighty shaft, was motionless and silent.

The brook—Green Brook—released from its bondage and servitude went freely and joyfully on its way, sparkling and dancing in the sunlight, singing its Sabbath song of praise and gladness, as it rippled on over its stony bed, or turned aside in circling eddies into some deep pool among the lily pads, or under the overhanging alders, to gossip with the fishes, as it went or its way to the sea rejoicing.

To the east, the south, and the west, the Plain spread out to the horizon's verge, a panorama of pastoral beauty.

In places the wooded groves, and the great apple orchards, then abundant hereabouts, marked the landscape with the dark green of their foliage.

Interspersed with these were fields of sturdy corn and yellow grain, waving in the sunshine and the gentle breezes, and prophesying to the waiting farmer of the coming harvest.

The meadows, too, which carpeted with their verdure most of the Plain, were bright and worshipful with their bloom and with their fragrance, which under the wooing of the warm sunbeams and the inborn impulses of their own nature, were exhaled as the incense of gratitude and love for the Great Creator of the mountains mighty and lilies of the valley fair and frail.

The hush and calm was broken, not disturbed by the neighing of horses and the lowing of the kine in the distance. Overhead in the branches of the trees, the song-birds were filling the air with the melody of their songs of praise and happiness, while all around there came to the ear the monotonous hum and drone of the bee and insect, which served to soothe the mind and give added repose to the Baptism of tranquility, which typified the angels' song at the Saviour's birth, "Peace on earth, good will to men."

Over all this scene of peaceful beauty from the "delectable hills" to the "sweet fields" then "dressed in living green," the overhanging canopy of blue and gold, seemed to come down nearer to earth and enfold within its radiant curtains, for the time at least, this quiet spot; and it needed but a slight effort of the imagination to give to the listening ear of the devout soul "the still, small voice" of the Christ whispering through the Heavenly corridors: "Come unto me, all ye that labor and are heavy laden, and I will give you rest."

And with one accord the people all went into the Temple for Worship.

When all were seated, the Minister arose, while every head was bowed, returned thanks to God for all the mercies which we enjoyed, and invoked the Divine blessing upon the services of the day and for guidance to words and thoughts and feelings of preacher and people.

The hymn was then given out:

"Majestic Sweetness sits Enthroned
"Upon the Savior's brow;
"His head with radiant glory crowned,
"His lips with grace o'erflow."

This hymn was the keynote to the service of the day. We knew that the message would come from Calvary, and not from Sinai, and when the words of the hymn went out upon the voices of the Congregation on the tune of Ortonville, the hearts of the people were as one with themselves and their preacher—receptive, loving, worshipful.

We had in those days no "Service of Song," by that name, we had no responsive readings of the Scriptures, no Antiphonal Service of any kind.

The Minister read the Scriptures and the hymns, the Precentor "led the singing," and his leading was followed by the Congregation with willing tongue, and with tuneful voice, and lofty praise.

No trained Choir awed or amazed the people, or drove the very idea of worship out of mind, by its skill and perfection in vocal calisthenics or sometimes gymnastics.

But the singers of those days, while not always precisely in tune or "on time," sang with the hallowed inspiration of praise, gratitude, and reverence for Him whom they were taught to regard as Creator, Benefactor, Saviour.

When the hymn had been sung and the hearts of the people were attuned to the sweetness of harmony and of love for the subject of the hymn, who had so loved them, the Minister then began reading the Scripture lesson.

This consisted of selections from the Sermon on the Mount, including the golden rule, and the Beatitudes.

From this treasure-house of the Wisdom and love of the Master, so much was given as was needful to prepare the minds of the listeners for further consideration of the subject-matter of the coming sermon.

Following the reading, the Hymn announced was,

"All hail the power of Jesus' name
"Let Angels prostrate fall;
"Bring forth the royal diadem,
"And Crown Him Lord of all."

This crowning of Christ, borne aloft upon the exultant strains of "Coronation," gave grand outlet and utterance to the rising warmth of the devotional spirit which was overcoming the assembly.

When this glad song of acclaim had ended, it's triumphant ascriptions of Kingship and Lordship to the Christ, and it's expressions of loyalty to Him as Prince and King and Saviour, had been wafted into upper air, and upward toward the heavenly throne, and the listening Ear Divine;

then were the worshippers, the ready, rapt, eager listeners to the words of the Preacher, as he gave out the text:

"Behold the Lamb of God, which taketh away the sins of the World."

And now we knew, of a truth, that this day's message was the voice from Calvary, not from Sinai.

The Preacher was in his kindliest mood. His heart, as well as his head was in, and behind what he said. He sought to unravel no theological entanglements. He simply preached "Christ and Him crucified."

Beginning at the Manger cradle, in the cavern of the Khan at Bethlehem, whither the Star had guided the Magi, and found them kneeling awe-stricken and worshipful, worshipping before the Child, whom they had been told in a vision, was "born King of the Jews;" and unto whom they were gladly giving gifts of gold, frankincense, and myrrh, and homage-worship as well; the preacher went skilfully over many of the prominent events in the life of the Nazarene, selecting such as pointed most directly to His Divine Humanity, showing Him as a "Man of sorrows, and acquainted with grief" and, as at the baptismal waters of the Jordan, when the hovering Dove brooded over the example set by Jesus for his followers, and the voice of Deity spake from above to a listening world: "This is my beloved Son in whom I am well pleased; hear ye him."

The Preacher then illustrated some traits in the dual character borne by this "Son of Joseph, the carpenter."

His poverty and humility, as when he said: "The foxes have holes and the birds of the air have nests, but the Son of Man, hath not where to lay his head."

His power and sublimity; as when he spake to the winds, and the tempest on the Sea of Galilee, and the turbulent waves obeyed the Master's voice, and sank to calm again.

But of all the characteristics displayed in the life of Him "who spake as never man spake," the Preacher dwelt longest and most emphatically upon the Love displayed in all the Saviour's works and ways.

How He fed the hungry, healed the sick, opened deaf ears, gave sight to the blind, cleansed the lepers, raised the dead.

How he strove to teach by word and Example the heaven-born lesson of the Golden Rule, and the parable of the Good Samaritan.

Tracing the earthly career of the Christ, from Bethlehem to Calvary, he pointed out how in all that life of majesty, omnipotence and God-likeness, all those attributes and potencies which marked Him as the Son of God, were in turn subordinated to unwearied self-abnegation, and to the most untiring ministration of goodness, mercy and love; the preacher strove to win his hearers to imitate in their lives, and towards each other, as men and brethren, in their daily intercourse the sublime example of their "elder brother, their intercessor," "the Lamb of God which taketh away the sins of the World."

The peroration covered with graphic fidelity and eloquence the last crowning act of self-sacrificing love for man—the tragic scene, when the sun was darkened, and night at mid day brooded over the rent, and reeling earth, and suspended on the Cross, the Saviour, with compassion more than mortal, prayed for His persecutors: "Father for-"give them for they know not what they do;" and the curtain fell upon that awful scene, as the same voice exclaimed: "It is finished."

Pity, gratitude and love for and to the Christ filled all hearts.

But high above all these emotions arose the sense of triumph in His triumph, the glow of joy inexpressible in His conquest—the feeling of victory born of His last triumphant words: "It is finished."

And these high-born and holy sentiments welling up and overflowing in their hearts, were relieved but not fully expressed in the closing hymn set to the tune of "Merdin."

"Burst ye Emerald gates and bring
"To my raptured vision,
"All the Exstatic joys that spring
"'Round the bright Elysian:
"Lo! we lift our longing eyes,
"Break, ye intervening skies.
"Sun of Righteousness, arise,
"Ope the gates of Paradise.
"Sweetest sound in Seraphs' song,
"Sweetest sound on Mortal's tongue;
"Sweetest carol ever sung—
"Let it's Echoes flow along."

When the voice of song in these exultant strains, were gradually led by the Precentor to the words of long metre doxology—

"Praise God from whom all blessings flow,
Praise Him all Creatures here below;
Praise Him above, ye heavenly host,
Praise Father, Son, and Holy Ghost"—

which was rendered upon the majestic measures of "Old Hundred," the worshippers were well prepared to receive from the good Minister's lips the Benediction, and retire from the house, with refreshed souls, and devout hearts, hoping to be thereby helped to do good and get good, in the coming week, convinced, as they were, that Love is the grand remedy for all social evils, as it is, indeed, the only foundation for good, toward God or Man.

And so they went out, and only stopping to bid each other affectionate adieus, they separated and went to their several homes.

In the evening the villagers, and a few from the suburbs, met in the upper room of the Old School House and had a simple service.

The Pastor or Deacon Hetfield, or Alexander Wilson, would read a selection from the scriptures, and make a brief exposition of it. Prayers were offered and hymns sung, and with exhortations to believers and unbelievers, the meeting would close and the people return to their homes. A most delightful feature of those "evening meetings" and one over which memory lingers with fondness, was the singing led by Mr. William Drake, son of Nathaniel, assisted by Miss Margaretta Osborn, sister of the late Sheriff, Joseph Manning Osborn; and when the songs of praise led by their young, clear and melodious voices, it was no mere "lip service" but bore aloft the very sign of true Praise. They are now for a half century or more, husband and wife, living happily at Irvington, and members of the Baptist Church at Lyons Farms.

And thus ended a Mid-Summer Sabbath at Scotch Plains, fifty years, and more ago.

This Sketch must close, as it began:

"Not many will come up to our Sesqui Centennial Anniversary who were here at the date of this sketch, which is Ante-Centennial."